# TAPAS

## MEXICAN AND SPANISH STARTERS, SOUPS AND SNACKS

**Angus&Robertson**
An imprint of HarperCollins*Publishers*

**An Angus & Robertson Publication**
Angus&Robertson, an imprint of
HarperCollins Publishers
25 Ryde Road, Pymble, Sydney NSW 2073, Australia
31 View Road, Glenfield, Auckland 10, New Zealand
77–85 Fulham Palace Road, London W6 8JB, United Kingdom
10 East 53rd Street, New York NY 10022, USA
First published in Australia in 1994

National Library of Australia
Cataloguing-in-Publication data:
Tapas: Mexican and Spanish starters, soups and snacks.
ISBN 0207 18605 7.
1. Appetisers. 2. Cookery, Spanish. 3. Cookery, Mexican. 641.812

Additional text by Pamela Allardice
Design by Liz Seymour
Illustrations by Penny Lovelock
Photography by Ashley Mackevicius
Food Styling by Anneka Mitchell
Printed in Hong Kong

9 8 7 6 5 4 3 2 1
97 96 95 94

# CONTENTS

## Introduction 5

## Salsas

## Aperitivos

## Soups

## Antojitos

## Salads

## Index 56

# INTRODUCTION

**THE MEXICANS AND SPANISH LOVE AN EXCUSE TO HAVE
A PARTY AND DELIGHT IN FEASTING AT A TAPAS BAR
OR CAFE, WHERE A SUMPTUOUS ARRAY OF APPETISERS
AND SNACKS WILL BE ON OFFER.**

In fact, tapas is much more an eating event than the cocktail party tends to be in most countries. It begins early evening when the satisfaction of the heavy noon meal has worn off, and continues until ten at night — when it is time for a late supper.

When the Spanish conquered Mexico more than 400 years ago they not only found gold, but also corn, beans, chillies, tomatoes, avocados, potatoes, squash, zucchinis and a wealth of new fruits and spices.

When they returned to Spain with their booty, local chefs hastened to imitate the cuisine that had been satisfying Mexican palates for centuries. These ingredients are now to be found in the full range of Mexican and Spanish cuisine, including braised meats, poultry and vegetables, tempting salads, as well as the famous tapas. For the most part, tapas snacks are fresh, mouthwatering toppings on a variety of corn bases and pastries and served with spicy salsas, all designed to tantalise the appetite.

# SALSAS

**NO FEAST IS COMPLETE WITHOUT AT LEAST ONE OR TWO SALSAS ON THE TABLE. THEY ARE SPOONED OVER MEAT DISHES, TACOS, EGGS AND BEANS; SERVED AS DIPS WITH *TOTOPOS* (TORTILLA CHIPS) OR CORN CHIPS, OR POURED OVER ENCHILADAS BEFORE BAKING.**

S ome are made raw to be served immediately like the famous avocado sauce, Salsa de Guacamole, or the fresh tomato, onion and chilli sauce, Salsa Cruda. Others are cooked sauces like Pepita Seed Sauce, a fiery condiment to be kept on hand for many meals to come.

The Aztec word for sauce was molli — hence 'mole' — the range of sauces served at Montezuma's table. You will find recipes for moles in this chapter, although we have mostly concentrated on the sauces that are derived from the Mexican salsa or sauce.

Salsas appear on every tapas table, and with every meal as a condiment for fish, meats, tacos and enchiladas or as a dip for corn chips or tortillas.

The essential herbs and spices that give salsas their zing are oregano, coriander, cumin, cloves and chilli powder. Occasionally you will need paprika, aniseed or turmeric. The main fresh herbs for authentic salsas are coriander and parsley, both of which are readily available. A tip to make them last longer: store fresh herbs in a jar of water covered with a plastic bag in your refrigerator.

# Fresh Red Tomato and Chilli Sauce

*Salsa Cruda*

**3 tomatoes, peeled, seeded
and chopped
2 to 3 fresh, large, hot red chillies,
seeded and finely chopped
1 onion, peeled and finely chopped
½ teaspoon sugar
2 teaspoons lime or lemon juice
2 tablespoons finely chopped fresh
coriander**

**1** Combine all the ingredients except coriander in a bowl. Cover and stand for at least 1 hour to allow the flavours to develop fully.
**2** Stir through coriander and season to taste with freshly ground black pepper and salt.
**3** Store in an airtight container in the refrigerator where it will keep for up to 1 week.

***Makes 1½ cups (375 ml/12 fl oz)***

On a hot day, serve this sauce chilled over a colourful cocktail of prawns and oysters.

# Green Chilli Sauce

*Salsa Verde*

**1 onion, peeled and finely chopped
2 tablespoons vegetable oil
2½ cups (550 g/18 oz) cooked
or canned tomatillos, drained
1 tablespoon finely chopped
fresh coriander
2 green California chillies or any
large medium to hot green chillies
1 cup (250 ml/8 fl oz) chicken stock
1 clove garlic, crushed (optional)**

**1** Place all ingredients in a food processor or blender and process until smooth.
**2** Transfer to a saucepan, season to taste with freshly ground black pepper and salt and simmer for 10 minutes or until sauce reaches desired consistency.

***Makes 3 cups (750 ml/24 fl oz)***

### TORTILLAS

Throughout this book, the reference to tortillas is exclusively in regard to the soft Mexican corn bread. There is also the Spanish tortilla, a delicious potato omelette, which is often served as a tapas dish in its own right, cut in thick wedges and served cold.

# Avocado Dip

*Guacamole*

**2 large ripe avocados, stoned
and peeled
2 teaspoons finely chopped onions
1 garlic clove, crushed
2 tablespoons lemon or lime juice
½ teaspoon salt
1 tomato, peeled, seeded and finely
chopped
2 tablespoons sour cream or
mayonnaise**

**2 teaspoons finely chopped fresh
coriander (optional)
1 to 3 hot red chillies (depending on
taste), seeded and finely chopped or
½ teaspoon chilli powder (optional)**

**1** Mash avocados with a fork. Add
remaining ingredients and mix well
to combine.
**2** Serve in a wooden or stone bowl
with wedges of tomato and corn
chips, garnished with coriander
leaves.

*Makes 2 cups (500 ml)*

# HOT CHILLIS

Chillis, chilli powder and chilli oil are basic ingredients for the recipes in this book. Even very simple tapas dishes, such as herbed olives or salads may be enhanced with that extra touch of chilli, or preserved or pickled chillies. In warm weather, eating food enhanced with chillis will brighten up any meal and add an extra touch of spice to a barbeque or picnic. Sprinkle chilli powder over corn on the cob grilled with garlic butter, or marinated chicken wings for something rather special.

One of the more popular uses for chillis and chilli sauces is as an appetiser before the main meal. Serve the chilli sauce of your choice with marinated anchovies, spiced pepita seeds and goat's cheese that has been marinated with tarragon and garlic. These highly flavoured tapas dishes will stimulate the appetite while still leaving room for something more substantial.

# Red Enchilada Sauce

*Enchilada Salsa Roja*

**3 tablespoons olive oil**
**2 tablespoons plain flour**
**or instant masa**
**chilli powder**
**pinch dried oregano**
**pinch ground cumin**
**2 cloves garlic, crushed**
**2 cups (500 ml/16 fl oz) tomato purée**
**1 cup (250 ml/8 fl oz) chicken stock**

**1** Heat oil in a saucepan. Add flour, chilli powder, oregano and cumin and cook over a medium heat, stirring constantly, until golden brown. Add garlic and tomato purée and mix to combine.
**2** Stir the stock into the tomato and chilli mixture and bring to the boil, reduce heat and simmer for 10 minutes, or until sauce reaches the desired consistency. Store in an airtight container in the refrigerator for up to two weeks.

***Makes 3 cups (750 ml/24 fl oz)***

# Ranch Style Chilli Sauce

*Salsa Ranchera*

**1 onion, peeled and chopped**
**2 cloves garlic, crushed**
**4 large ripe tomatoes, peeled**
**1 cup (185 g/6 oz) canned**
**jalapeño chillies**
**½ teaspoon dried oregano**
**1 tablespoon finely chopped**
**fresh parsley**

**1** Place all ingredients in a food processor or blender and process until fairly smooth.
**2** Transfer to a saucepan, bring to the boil, reduce heat and simmer for 10 to 15 minutes or until sauce reaches desired consistency.
**3** Stand for at least 2 hours before serving to allow flavours to develop fully.

***Makes 2 cups (310 g/10 oz)***

# Red Chilli Sauce

*Salsa Roja*

**170 g (6 oz) fresh hot red
chillies, seeded**
**3 cups (750 ml/24 fl oz) hot water**
**3 tablespoons tomato paste**
**1 garlic clove, crushed**
**3 tablespoons olive oil**
**pinch salt**
**¼ teaspoon ground cumin**
**1 teaspoon finely chopped fresh
oregano**
**1 teaspoon finely chopped fresh
coriander**

**1** Rinse chillies in cool water. Place in a bowl, cover with hot water and allow to soak for 1 hour. (Alternately, steam them for 5 minutes.)

**2** Place chillies and remaining ingredients in a food processor or blender with a little extra water and process until coarsely chopped.

**3** Place mixture in a saucepan and simmer slowly for 10 minutes, stirring occasionally, or until sauce reaches the desired consistency.

*Makes 3½ cups (875 ml/1½ pints)*

# TOMATOES

Both simple tapas and the more exotic and complicated recipes invariably rely on the informal and versatile tomato. Tomato-based tapas are a delight for vegetarians as they provide plenty of punchy taste without relying on meat or its by-products. Some favourite combinations are tomatoes with garlic, tomatoes with beans and, of course, tomatoes with capsicums and chilli peppers.

Try tiny cherry tomatoes as tapas snacks in their own right — fill them with a mixture of tuna and basil, or chicken mince and hard-boiled egg. Wrap them in bacon and drizzle sour cream over them. Or, halve them and cook them lightly with zucchini and capsicum strips and serve as a show-stopping filling for empanadas.

## TOMATILLOS

Tomatillo, also known as 'husk tomato' or green tomato, is not an ordinary tomato. Each one is surrounded by a husky, papery leaf and the fruit often appears to be glued into the leaf because of the sap this unusual tropical plant excretes. Tomatillos are zesty in flavour when eaten raw; when cooked they lose their acidic taste but retain their slightly lemony flavour. They are excellent as a sauce, in guacamole, or to flavour meat dishes. Raw tomatillos look great as a garnish and make a wonderful conversation piece on a plate of appetisers. They are widely available canned outside Mexico and Spain.

# Fresh Green Chilli Sauce

*Salsa Verde Fresca*

**1½ cups (330 g/11 oz) canned tomatillos, drained and finely chopped**
**1 onion, peeled and finely chopped**
**1 clove garlic, crushed**
**2 fresh or canned large hot green chillies, seeded and finely chopped**
**1 green capsicum (pepper), finely chopped**
**½ teaspoon freshly ground black pepper**
**¼ teaspoon salt**
**pinch sugar**
**1 tablespoon lime juice**
**2 tablespoons finely chopped fresh coriander**

**1** Combine all ingredients in a bowl, cover and allow to stand for at least 1 hour before serving.

**Makes about 3 cups (750 ml/24 fl oz)**

VARIATION: *For a smooth Fresh Green Chilli Sauce, place ingredients in a food processor or blender and process until smooth. To serve, sprinkle with extra chopped fresh coriander.*

14

# Avocado Sauce

*Salsa de Guacamole*

**2 tablespoons pepitas**
**2 to 3 medium to hot green chillies,**
**steamed and peeled**
**small bunch fresh parsley,**
**finely chopped**
**2 tablespoons finely chopped**
**fresh coriander**
**3 tablespoons vegetable oil**
**⅓ cup (80 ml/2½ fl oz)**
**chicken stock**
**3 avocados, stoned, peeled**
**and mashed**

**1** Place pepitas, chillies, parsley and coriander in a food processor or blender and process until finely chopped. Add a little chicken stock and strain, reserving chilli mixture.
**2** Heat oil in a frypan and cook chilli mixture for 1 minute. Add remaining stock, bring to boil, reduce heat and simmer for 5 minutes.
**3** Set aside and allow to cool. Add avocado and mix until smooth.

***Makes 2 to 3 cups***
***(500 to 750 ml/16 to 24 fl oz)***

# Pepita Seed Sauce

*Salsa de Pepita*

**100 g (3½ oz) pepitas, toasted**
**2 fresh small green chillies, seeded**
**small bunch fresh parsley,**
**finely chopped**
**2 cups (500 ml/16 fl oz) chicken stock**

**1** Place pepitas, chillies, parsley and stock in a food processor or blender and process until smooth.
**2** Transfer to a saucepan, bring to the boil and cook for 1 minute, stirring constantly, or until heated through and well combined.

***Makes 2 cups (500 ml/16 fl oz)***

# Cheese Sauce for Tortilla Chips

*Salsa de Queso*

1 cup (250 g/8 oz) Ricotta cheese
125 g (4 oz) Cheddar cheese, grated
½ cup (125 ml/4 fl oz) sour cream
½ teaspoon ground cumin
pinch dried oregano
1 fresh small chilli, seeded and finely
chopped or ¼ teaspoon chilli powder
1 tomato, peeled, seeded
and finely chopped

**1** In the top of a double saucepan, melt the Ricotta, Cheddar cheese and sour cream over simmering water, stirring occasionally.
**2** Add cumin, oregano, chilli and freshly ground black pepper to taste. Cook 2 to 3 minutes longer or until heated through and well combined.
**3** Fold in the tomato, heat through and serve immediately with tortilla chips.

*Makes 3 cups (750 ml/24 fl oz)*

# Avocado and Onion Dip

*Guacamole Sencillo*

3 large ripe avocados, stoned
and peeled
1 medium onion, peeled and
finely chopped
2 hot red chillies, seeded
and finely chopped
⅓ cup (80 ml/2½ fl oz) lemon juice
dash Tabasco sauce
1 tablespoon chopped coriander

**1** Mash avocados with a fork. Add remaining ingredients, season to taste with freshly ground black pepper and salt and mix well to combine.
**2** Garnish with chopped fresh coriander and serve with tortilla chips if desired.

*Makes 2 cups (500 ml/16 fl oz)*

# APERITIVOS

**FOLLOWING HUNDREDS OF YEARS OF TRADITION, EATING *APERITIVOS* OR SNACKS IS PART OF THE DAILY ROUTINE FOR MEXICANS AND SPANIARDS. ANYTIME FROM 11 AM ONWARDS, PEOPLE WILL HEAD FOR THEIR FAVOURITE BAR OR CAFE AND, IN KEEPING WITH THE IMPORTANCE OF THE RITUAL, ORDER THEIR FAVOURITE *APERITIVO* AND A DRINK.**

They will then experiment with whatever new delicacies the proprietor may have on offer.

As a result of centuries of Moorish occupation, many of these Spanish snacks have Arab overtones. In addition, many of the foods brought back from the New World (potatoes, capsicums and tomatoes, for instance) will be found. Several 'pan' or bread recipes are also popular, including the *bolillo* or French roll, which is the basis for *tortas*, or submarine sandwiches. Yeast breads are often served as a snack or, like Pan de Muerto (Bread of the Dead), as a special treat for a festive day in Mexico.

Chillies, onions, garlic, cucumbers, lettuce and other salad greens, avocados, sweet corn and zucchini (courgettes) are all excellent standbys for preparing tasty *aperitivos*, as are fresh limes, lemons and oranges, grated cheese, fresh eggs, canned tomatoes, tomato paste and purée. Cans of beans and corn are also useful as are green olives, pepitas (pumpkin seeds), peanuts and pine nuts, dried beans, dried chillies and white long-grain rice.

# Seasoned Jalapeño Chillies

*Jalapeños con Espices*

**3 tablespoons lemon pepper**
**3 tablespoons coarse salt**
**1 cup (185 g/6 oz) canned jalapeño**
**chillies, drained**
**1 small onion, peeled and thinly sliced**
**into rings (optional)**

**1** Combine lemon pepper and salt.
Place in the centre of a serving plate
and arrange chillies and onion rings.

**Serves 4**

A very basic utensil in the Spanish kitchen is the
mortar and pestle. Despite the availability of modern
food processors, it is still frequently used to grind
nuts, spices and garlic.

# Tortilla Chips

*Totopos Fritos*

**12 fresh and soft corn tortillas,**
**quartered**
**vegetable oil for cooking**
**salt to taste**

**1** Heat oil in a heavy-based pan and
cook tortilla pieces until golden and
crisp. Drain on absorbent paper.
**2** Sprinkle with salt to taste, allow
to cool and serve with your
favourite salsa or guacamole.

NOTE: *The tortillas can be salted before they
are cooked. Brush both sides with a mixture of
2 teaspoons of salt and 3 tablespoons of water.
Set aside and allow to dry completely before
cooking.*

**Serves 4**

# Soused Oysters

*Ostiones en Escabeche*

24 large fresh oysters in half shell
⅓ cup (80 ml/2½ fl oz) fresh
lemon juice
⅓ cup (80 ml/2½ fl oz) fresh
lime juice
1 tablespoon orange juice
½ teaspoon dried oregano
sprig fresh marjoram, finely chopped
or ¼ teaspoon dried marjoram
3 black peppercorns
2 cloves garlic
1 bay leaf
⅓ cup (80 ml/2½ fl oz) olive oil
⅓ cup (80 ml/2½ fl oz) dry
white wine
6 canned small chillies, finely
chopped, or 6 fresh small chillies,
steamed and finely chopped
1 onion, peeled and finely chopped
1 tablespoon chopped fresh parsley
1 tablespoon chopped fresh coriander
crushed ice

**1** Remove the oysters from their shells and set aside. Clean shells and reserve.
**2** Place lemon, lime and orange juices, oregano, marjoram, peppercorns and garlic in a saucepan and gently bring to the boil. Remove from heat immediately and cool slightly.
**3** Heat oil in a frypan and lightly sauté oysters. Drain on absorbent paper.
**4** Combine wine, chillies and onion in a bowl. Add warm lemon and lime mixture and oysters, and stir gently. Cover and allow to marinate in the refrigerator for 3 hours or overnight.
**5** To serve: Spoon oyster mixture into reserved shells, sprinkle with parsley and coriander and place shells on a bed of crushed ice.

*Serves 4*

# Savoury Toasted Pepitas

*Pepitas Tostada*

30 g (1 oz) butter or margarine
1 to 2 cloves garlic, crushed
¼ teaspoon chilli powder
250 g (8 oz) pepitas
1 tablespoon Worcestershire sauce

**1** Melt butter in a large heavy-based pan and cook garlic and chilli powder over medium heat for 1 minute.
**2** Add pepitas and cook, stirring constantly, until they have all popped. Add Worcestershire sauce and mix well to combine. Season to taste with salt if desired.
**3** Serve warm or cold.

*Makes 250 g (8 oz)*

# Spicy Empanadas

*Empanadas de Picadillo*

*Empanadas are little pastry turnovers stuffed with savoury or sweet fillings. In Mexico and Spain, empanadas are sold by street vendors, in markets and at* panadarias. *The savoury ones are often served with a red or a green chilli sauce.*

**750 g (24 oz) readymade
shortcrust pastry
vegetable oil for cooking**
FILLING
**2 teaspoons oil
1 clove garlic, crushed
250 g (8 oz) minced beef
250 g (8 oz) minced pork
½ cup (125 ml/4 fl oz) tomato purée
⅓ cup (80 ml/2½ fl oz) sherry
1 teaspoon ground allspice
1 teaspoon ground cumin
1 teaspoon ground cinnamon
½ teaspoon ground cloves
1 tablespoon sugar
1 tablespoon freshly squeezed lime
or lemon juice
125 g (4 oz) slivered almonds**

**1** To make filling: heat oil in a pan and cook garlic for 1 minute. Add beef and pork and cook over a medium high heat for 4 to 5 minutes or until browned. Add tomato purée, sherry, allspice, cumin, cinnamon, cloves, sugar and lime juice. Reduce heat and simmer, uncovered, for 20 minutes, stirring occasionally, until most of the liquid evaporates. Add almonds and set aside to cool.

**2** Roll pastry out to 3 mm (¼ in) thickness and cut out ten 12 cm (5 in) circles, using an upturned saucer as a guide.

**3** Place a spoonful of mixture on one side of each pastry round. Moisten pastry edges with a little water. Fold over to enclose and press edges firmly together with a fork to seal.

**4** Heat enough oil in a deep pan to cover base by 3 cm to 5 cm (1 to 2 in) and cook pastries for 4 to 5 minutes or until golden brown and cooked through. Alternatively, bake at 190°C (375°F) for 15 to 20 minutes.

**5** Serve with Red or Green Chilli Sauce.

*Serves 4*

### SWEET EMPANADAS
Substitute meat fillings with jams, preserves, mincemeat, or a sweet filling of your choice. Prepare empanadas as above and sprinkle tops with sugar before baking.

# Corn Bread

*Pan de Maíz*

**60 g (2 oz) butter**
**1 onion, peeled and finely chopped**
**1 to 2 fresh small chillies,**
**finely chopped**
**1 egg**
**1 cup (250 ml/8 fl oz) milk**
**1 cup (250 g/8 oz) creamed corn**
**1 cup (175 g/6 oz) polenta (cornmeal)**
**1 cup (125 g/4 oz) plain flour**
**1½ teaspoons baking powder**
**1 teaspoon salt**
**60 g (2 oz) Cheddar cheese, grated**

**1** Melt butter in a frypan and cook onion and chilli over a medium heat for 3 to 4 minutes or until onion is soft. Set aside.
**2** Whisk together egg and milk. Add corn and mix well.
**3** Sift together polenta, flour, baking powder and salt into a mixing bowl. Add chilli mixture, egg mixture and cheese and mix until just combined.
**4** Spoon into a greased and lined 20 cm (8 in) square cake pan and bake at 180°C (350°F) for 30 to 35 minutes or until golden and cooked when tested with a skewer.

***Serves 4***

# The Devil's Sandwich

*Torta Diablo*

*These very hot delights are popular in the markets of the older Spanish cities, such as Toledo.*

**50 g (2 oz) butter or margarine**
**6 large French or Italian bread rolls,**
**split in half**
**2 cups (500 g/16 oz) shredded**
**cooked beef, chicken or pork**
**1 small onion, peeled and finely**
**chopped**
**3 cups (750 ml/24 fl oz) Red Chilli**
**Sauce**

**1** Melt butter or margarine in pan and cook rolls on each side over a medium heat until golden brown. Remove and set aside to keep warm.
**2** Add shredded meat to pan and cook until heated through. Place cooked meat on the bottom half of the rolls, sprinkle with onion and top with roll.
**3** Quickly dip the whole roll in warmed Red Chilli Sauce and serve immediately, accompanied by jalapeño chillies and shredded lettuce, if desired.

***Serves 6***

# Bread of the Dead

*Pan de Muerto*

**1 teaspoon dried yeast**
**3 tablespoons warm water**
**4 cups plain flour, sifted**
**1 teaspoon salt**
**⅓ cup (50 g/2 oz) caster sugar**
**125 g (4 oz) butter or margarine, cut into pieces**
**1 tablespoon finely grated orange rind**
**1 tablespoon finely grated lime or lemon rind**
**6 eggs, lightly beaten**

**1** Dissolve yeast in warm water. Cover and set aside in a draught-free place for 5 to 10 minutes or until mixture is frothy.

**2** Sift flour, salt and sugar together into a bowl. Rub in butter with fingertips until mixture resembles fine breadcrumbs. Stir through orange and lemon rinds. Make a well in the centre and add yeast mixture and eggs. Mix to a soft dough.

**3** Turn onto a floured surface and knead for 5 minutes or until smooth and elastic. Place dough in a large greased bowl, cover with plastic wrap and set aside in a warm draught-free place for 1 to 1¼ hours, or until doubled in bulk.

**4** Turn onto a floured surface and knead for 2 minutes longer. Divide dough into 4 portions and separate a small ball from each portion. This will become the 'bones' to decorate the bread.

**5** Shape the four large portions into balls and place on a greased and floured oven tray. Flatten slightly with palm of hand. Shape smaller portions of dough each into 2 'bones'. Brush surface of larger portions lightly with water and place 'bones' on top to form crossbones.

**6** Cover with plastic wrap and set aside in a warm, draught-free place for 45 to 60 minutes or until a fingerprint pressed into the dough remains. Bake at 180°C (350°F) for 30 to 35 minutes, or until golden brown and bread sounds hollow when tapped on the base with fingertips.

## BAKED CORN CHIPS

If you like freshly made corn chips but are mindful of calories and cholesterol, bake them instead of deep frying them.

# FOODSTUFFS

Prepared *fajita* (meat strips), marinades, dried chillies, bottled salsas and other manufactured Spanish products are available at Mexican and Spanish food suppliers and in the exotic food sections of major department stores. Cans of the many varieties of chillies, tomatillos (green tomatoes), nopales (pickled pear leaves), pimiento, hominy (a type of corn for soup) and pastes or powders like *mole pablano*, are exported from Mexico and Spain and are usually of excellent quality. Even good cooks in those countries use them!

Readymade corn and wheatflour tortillas can be bought by the dozen and frozen in batches to be used for future meals. They are avaliable from Mexican and Spanish food suppliers or tortilla factories, which supply local Mexican and Spanish restaurants. Phone your local restaurant and ask them where you can buy fresh tortillas. Otherwise they are sometimes available frozen at some larger supermarkets.

# SOUPS

**SOUP OFTEN SIGNALS THE START OF A MAIN MEAL, AND IN MEXICO AND SPAIN IT IS IN THE EARLY AFTERNOON, BEFORE SIESTA. SOUPS ARE ALSO DELICIOUS TAPAS DISHES, AND ARE DESIGNED TO PRIME YOUR APPETITE FOR THE FEAST TO COME.**

There are two kinds of soup. Wet soups (*sopas aguadas*) are like the soups most Westerners are used to. Dry soups (*sopas secas*) are rice or noodle dishes that have absorbed the soup stock or broth in which they were cooked. Many people can often begin with a *sopa aguada* and then follow with a *sopa seca*, before the main course.

There are exceptions. The following recipes include the famous *pozole*, the national favourite reflecting yet again the Mexican love of corn, and which is really a meal in itself. *Pozole* is more a supper dish than a starter, in fact.

It is handy to have chicken, fish and beef stocks and broths in the freezer. Home-made stock is a good basis for making these authentic soups and is downright essential for making soup when time is limited. Stock cubes are an acceptable substitution, although they may have a saltier flavour.

Traditionally, these soups are cooked in earthenware casseroles and claypots, called cazuelas and ollas. To season earthenware pots, rib them with garlic, then fill them with warm water to which you have added some oregano, thyme or bay leaves, then bake them in a moderate oven for several hours.

# Pork and Hominy Soup

*Pozole*

*This is a popular supper dish and is often served at fiestas to celebrate birthdays or weddings, or at Christmas time.*

**1 kg (2 lb) pork shoulder, cut into
large pieces
3 litres (5 pints) water
2 x 500 g (16 oz) cans hominy or
corn kernels, drained
2 onions, peeled and finely chopped
1 teaspoon salt
2 cups shredded cabbage, or 1 small
cabbage, shredded
8 spring onions, finely chopped
2 carrots, peeled and grated
2 tomatoes peeled, seeded
and finely chopped
3 radishes, chopped
3 limes, cut into wedges
3 fresh hot red or green chillies,
finely chopped
chilli sauce, readymade or homemade**

**1** Place pork, water, hominy, onion and salt in a large, heavy based saucepan. Bring to the boil, reduce heat and simmer for 2 to 3 hours, or until the meat is tender.

**2** Remove pork from soup and cool. Shred meat. Skim fat from surface of cooled soup. Return shredded meat to soup and reheat.

**3** Serve cabbage, spring onions, carrots, tomatoes, radishes, chillies, limes and chilli sauce in separate bowls for each person to serve themselves.

**Serves 6**

VARIATION: *Substitute 2 medium chickens or 1 small turkey for pork. When chicken and turkey are cooked, debone, then add meat to soup.*

### POZOLE

Hominy is prepared from large white dried corn kernels which are available canned at most good delicatessens. Cooked in a huge soup pot and left to simmer all day long, *Pozole* has many variations, which contain pork, turkey or chicken. In Mexico they use the pig's head for a full-flavoured stock. Sometimes ordinary corn is used instead of hominy.

# SWEET CORN

Corn, one of the famed 'treasures of the New World' which the Spanish brought back with them from Mexico in the 16th century, is still an integral part of Mexican and Spanish cookery.

Corn includes a wide range of varieties, the two most commonly available being sweet corn and baby corn. The whole dried kernels of corn are easily ground, and the resulting meal forms the basis of many delicious breads and biscuits, notably corn chips.

Fresh corn has a wonderfully distinct flavour and appears frequently in Mexican and Spanish cuisine, in stews, side dishes, salads, or eaten marinated and grilled or barbequed with garlic and butter as a tapas dish. If you are buying fresh corn, look for cobs with kernels that are firm, tender and brightly-coloured. Avoid any blemished or withered cobs.

# Gazpacho

1 tablespoon ground almonds
1 garlic clove, crushed
1 tablespoon olive oil
1 kg (2 lb) ripe tomatoes, peeled,
seeded and finely chopped
1 small onion, peeled and finely
chopped
1 small cucumber, finely diced
1 cup (250 ml/8 fl oz) tomato juice
2 tablespoons red wine vinegar
2 tablespoons fresh lime juice
3 tablespoons finely chopped
fresh parsley
2 tablespoons finely chopped
fresh coriander
GARNISH
fresh lime wedges
chopped serrano chillies
fresh coriander leaves

**1** Combine ground almonds, garlic
and oil to form a smooth paste.
**2** Place tomatoes in a bowl, add
almond paste and remaining
ingredients. Mix well, taking care
not to crush the tomatoes. Chill for
at least 2 hours before serving.
**3** Serve in individual bowls with a
small amount of ice. Accompany
with wedges of lime and sprinkle
with fresh chopped serrano chillies
and coriander leaves.

*Serves 4 to 6*

# Bean Soup

*Sopa de Frijoles*

1 cup (220 g/7 oz) pinto or kidney
beans, washed and soaked for 8 hours
6 cups (1.5 litres/2½ pints) water
1 onion, peeled and finely sliced
2 canned tomatoes, chopped
1 clove garlic, crushed
½ teaspoon dried oregano
1 teaspoon chilli powder
3 slices stale bread with
crusts removed, cubed and cooked
in garlic oil till golden

**1** Drain and place beans in a heavy-
based saucepan. Add enough water
to cover them. Bring to the boil,
reduce heat and simmer for 5 hours,
adding more water during cooking
when necessary.
**2** Add onion, tomatoes, garlic,
oregano and chilli powder after 2½
hours of cooking. Continue to
simmer.
**3** When beans are tender, strain,
reserving stock and place in a food
processor or blender with a little
stock and process until smooth.
**4** Return to pan with stock, and
reheat. Add some extra boiling
water if soup is too thick. To serve,
sprinkle with croutons, chopped
onions, and coriander.

*Serves 4*

# Chilled Avocado Soup

*Sopa de Agualate*

**3 large ripe avocados
1¼ cups (310 ml/10 fl oz) cream
½ cup (125 ml/4 fl oz) milk
1 cup (250 ml/8 fl oz) chicken stock
1½ tablespoons fresh lemon juice
Tabasco sauce, to taste
chopped fresh chives,
to garnish**

**1** Stone and peel avocados. Place in a food processor or blender with fresh cream, milk and chicken stock and process until smooth. Add lemon juice, Tabasco and freshly ground black pepper and salt. Process to combine.

**2** Refrigerate until well chilled. Serve in a large soup tureen. Garnish with chives or coriander leaves and accompany with a bowl of sour cream.

*Serves 4 to 6*

# SQUASH FLOWERS

Squash flowers that do not bear fruit are greatly prized by Mexicans for their brilliant colouring and delicate flavouring. When in season, these fresh squash or zucchini (courgette) flowers are often used in Mexican and Spanish cuisine, especially in soups and salads and as a garnish for casseroles. They can also be fried, stuffed or lightly braised, mixed with eggs in a fritatta, or used in all manner of tasty side dishes.

You need to cook squash flowers as soon as possible after picking. Otherwise you can buy them canned at specialty food outlets. Sometimes, in European neighbourhoods or at Italian specialty produce stores, very small zucchini are sold with the flowers still attached. These are considered a great delicacy by both the Mexicans and the Spanish, with the latter serving them lightly tossed in butter and sprinkled with crunchy garlic bread crumbs as a tapas dish.

# Squash Flower Soup

*Sopa de Flor de Calabaza*

**30 g (1 oz) squash or zucchini
(courgette) flowers, stems and
pistils removed
125 g (4 oz) butter
4 to 6 spring onions, finely chopped
2 garlic cloves, peeled and finely
chopped
4 serrano or birdseye chillies, seeded
and finely sliced
pinch dried marjoram
pinch dried thyme
pinch dried oregano
pinch dried epazote (optional)
1 tablespoon chopped fresh parsley
6 cups (1½ litres/ 2½ pints) chicken
stock
250 g (8 oz) lean chicken breast
fillets, cut into 1 cm (½ in) cubes
30 g (1 oz) button mushrooms,
finely sliced
2 cups (500 ml/16 fl oz) cream**

**1** Carefully rinse the squash or
zucchini flowers and shake off
excess water. Roughly chop and set
aside.

**2** Melt 60 g (2 oz) butter in a large
heavy-based frypan and cook spring
onions, garlic and chillies over a
medium heat for 2 minutes. Add
flowers and cook for 2 to 3 minutes
longer. Mix in dried herbs and
parsley and season with freshly
ground black pepper and salt.
Cover and simmer for 10 minutes.
**3** Heat stock in a large heavy-based
saucepan. Add flower mixture.
Bring slowly to the boil and simmer
over a low heat for 5 minutes. Set
aside.
**4** Melt remaining butter in a frypan
and cook chicken cubes for 2 to 3
minutes or until cooked through.
Drain on absorbent paper and set
aside.
**5** Add mushrooms to pan and cook
over a medium high heat for 2 to 3
minutes or until tender. Drain on
absorbent paper and set aside.
**6** Reheat the stock and flower
mixture and add the chicken and
mushrooms. Season to taste with
freshly ground black pepper and
salt and stir in cream. Serve
immediately.

*Serves 4*

# ANTOJITOS

**PROBABLY THE TYPE OF MEXICAN FOOD BEST KNOWN OUTSIDE OF MEXICO IS WHAT THE MEXICANS THEMSELVES CALL *ANTOJITOS* — 'LITTLE WHIMS' OR CRAVINGS.**

The word *antojito* literally means 'a capricious whim or desire', and these dishes which are mostly based on the tortilla corn dough, *masa*, are really traditional Mexican fast food, on sale at marketplaces and at fetes and bazaars. *Antojitos* also appear at the late evening meal of the day, when supper calls for 'just a little something' to finish the day.

The most popular *antojitos* — enchiladas, tacos and tamales — are the mainstay of Mexican restaurants around the world, but only a small part of the wide variety of Mexican food on offer in most Mexican households.

Your own kitchen will have everything you need to improvise when making Mexican *antojitos*, but there are some special utensils you can buy if you wish. One is a small cast iron tortilla press, which will simplify tortilla making at home. You can order a tortilla press though any Mexican restaurant supplier in major cities. The small investment is well worth while if you like to make Mexican food.

# Chicken Tacos

*Tacos de Pollo*

**12 soft tortillas**
**vegetable oil for cooking**
**1 green capsicum (pepper),**
**cut into thin strips**
**1 cup (250 ml/8 fl oz) sour cream**
FILLING
**2 cups minced cooked chicken, or 2**
**chicken breast fillets, cooked**
**and minced**
**⅓ cup (80 g/2½ oz) cream cheese**
**3 tablespoons blanched almonds,**
**chopped**
RED CHILLI SAUCE
**1½ tablespoons olive oil**
**1 spring onion, finely chopped**
**3 to 4 fresh or canned hot red chillies,**
**seeded and finely chopped**
**1 clove garlic, crushed**
**3 tablespoons tomato purée**

**1** To make filling: Combine chicken, cheese and almonds and mix well. Season to taste with freshly ground black pepper and salt.

**2** To make sauce: Heat olive oil in a saucepan and cook onion, chillies and garlic over a medium heat for 3 to 4 minutes or until onion is soft. Add tomato purée and simmer for a further 1 to 2 minutes.

**3** Heat vegetable oil in a saucepan and cook tortillas until softened. Spread each one with a spoonful of chicken mixture, roll up and secure with toothpick.

**4** Top each taco with a strip of green capsicum, and a band of sour cream and Red Chilli Sauce before serving.

NOTE: *Prepared taco shells may be substituted for the tortillas in this recipe if you wish.*

**Makes 12**

### TACOS

Traditionally, a taco is a heated tortilla folded over a bit of filling. Tortillas can be warmed to soften them and folded over the filling or deep fried into a taco shell (buy them readymade) with various fillings placed inside.

# CHICKEN

Almost every family in rural Mexico and Spain has a small clutch of chickens. Even in the city, chickens can be found on the patios of tenement slums and in the courtyards of middle class neighbourhoods. Behind the traffic noise there is an incessant background symphony of clucking chickens and crowing roosters from the early hours of the morning.

Chicken is everyday fare in Mexico and Spain. At fiesta time, the village landowners all contribute chickens for the communal feast in proportion to their property, and the chickens are barbequed, casseroled, steamed or fried and served with sauces, or rolled in tortillas for enchiladas or tacos.

# Cheesy Turnovers

*Quesadillas*

1 cup (125 g/4 oz) dried masa or
instant masa
½ cup (60 g/2 oz) plain flour, sifted
½ teaspoon baking powder
¼ teaspoon salt
½ cup (125 ml/4 fl oz) water
3 tablespoons milk
250 g (8 oz) mild Cheddar cheese,
finely grated or 250 g (8 oz) cooked
meat, bean or cheese mixture
of your choice
12 fresh, medium, hot green chillies,
trimmed, steamed, seeded and
chopped
oil for cooking

**1** Combine masa, plain flour, baking powder and salt in a bowl. Combine water and milk. Add to masa mixture and mix to form a dough. Knead on a lightly floured surface until smooth.
**2** Divide dough into 16 equal portions and shape into balls. Cover with plastic wrap or a damp tea towel.
**3** Using a tortilla press, place a 22 cm (8½ in) square of plastic wrap or waxed paper over bottom plate. Place a portion of dough on top, a little off centre towards the hinge,

and press with palm of hand to flatten a little. Cover with a second sheet of plastic wrap or waxed paper and close firmly, but not too hard. Remove tortilla from press and carefully peel away plastic.
**4** To keep tortillas soft, cover with a damp kitchen cloth until required.
**5** Place a spoonful of cheese or meat/cheese mixture on a tortilla and top with chilli. Fold tortilla in half and press edges together firmly with fingertips.
**6** Cover with a damp cloth and repeat with remaining dough and filling.
**7** Heat enough oil in a large saucepan to cover 3 cm (1 in) deep, heat to 180°C (350°F) and cook quesadillas, a few at a time, until golden brown. Drain on absorbent paper. Serve hot with salsa of your choice.

*Makes 16*

## TORTILLA PRESS

Patting the dough into neat rounds by hand is not so easy, but by using a tortilla press, a small heavy cast-iron press now available in most large Western cities, you can enjoy freshly made Mexican-style tortillas with a minimum of fuss.

# Tamales

**250 g (8 oz) butter or margarine**
**3 cups (625 g/21 oz) dried masa or instant masa**
**2 tablespoons baking powder**
**1 teaspoon salt**
**¾ cup (180 ml/6 fl oz) chicken stock**
**25 corn husks or 8 x 10 cm (3 x 4 in) parchment paper pieces**

**1** Beat the butter or margarine until light and fluffy. Combine the masa, baking powder and salt. Add stock and mix well. Add to margarine and continue to beat until creamy.

**2** Soak corn husks in cold water for 1 hour to moisten. Pat dry with absorbent paper. Carefully flatten each one, and spread a large spoonful of masa dough over husk leaving a 2 cm (¾ in) border at each end.

**3** Place filling of your choice, in a sausage shape, on top of spread masa dough and roll corn husks to enclose filling.

**4** Pinch ends together and tie with a shred of corn husk or string to seal.

**5** Stack tamales in a large steamer, being careful not to overcrowd, and cook gently over simmering water for 45 to 60 minutes or until cooked.

*Makes 20 Tamales*

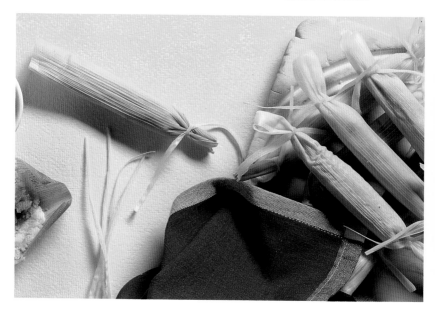

Place a spoonful of mixture along centre of tortilla, and carefully roll tortilla into a flute.

Holding the flute together with tongs, fry in hot oil until slightly crisp.

# Tortilla Flutes

*Flautas*

**2 tablespoons olive oil**
**1 small onion, peeled and finely chopped**
**1 garlic clove, crushed**
**1 teaspoon ground cumin**
**¼ teaspoon chilli powder**
**500 g (16 oz) cooked minced chicken**
**1 tablespoon finely chopped fresh coriander**
**vegetable oil for cooking**
**12 soft flour or corn tortillas**
**Red or Green Chilli Sauce**
**1 avocado, stoned, peeled and sliced**

**1** Heat olive oil in a frypan and cook onion and garlic over a medium heat for 2 to 3 minutes or until onion is just tender but not soft. Add chilli powder and cumin and cook for 1 minute.
**2** Stir through chicken. Cook over medium high heat until just heated through. Mix in coriander, remove from heat and set aside.
**3** Soften tortillas, one at a time, by heating in a dry heavy-based frypan over a high heat for about 30 seconds each side or dipping in hot oil.
**4** Lay tortilla flat and place a large spoonful of chicken mixture along centre of tortilla. Carefully roll the tortilla to form a flute.
**5** Heat enough oil in a deep frypan to cover 5 cm (2 in) deep.

Holding the flute together with tongs (or fasten with toothpicks) cook in hot oil until slightly crisp. Drain on absorbent paper. Repeat with remaining tortillas and filling.
**6** Serve with Red or Green Chilli Sauce and avocado slices.

*Serves 6*

# Savoury Chicken Tamale Filling

*Tamales de Pollo*

**¼ cup (60 ml/2 fl oz) olive or vegetable oil**
**¼ cup (30 g/1 oz) plain flour**
**1 clove garlic, crushed**
**1 small onion, peeled and chopped**
**2 tablespoons tomato purée**
**1 teaspoon dried oregano**
**500 g (16 oz) cooked chicken, shredded**
**⅓ cup (60 g/ 2 oz) blanched almonds**
**1 teaspoon chilli powder (optional)**

**1** Heat oil in a saucepan, stir in flour and cook over a medium heat, stirring constantly, until golden brown.
**2** Add garlic, onion, tomato purée, and oregano, reduce heat and simmer for 15 minutes. Stir through chicken and cook for 15 minutes longer. Set aside and allow to cool. Use to fill tamales.

*Makes enough for 20 tamales*

# SALADS

**IN MEXICO AND SPAIN, RATHER THAN SERVE VEGETABLES AS A DISH IN THEIR OWN RIGHT, THEY ARE OFTEN DISGUISED AS PART OF A MEAT OR SEAFOOD TAPAS DISH. THEY COULD BE CREAMED, FRIED OR STUFFED, OR BRAISED AND COVERED IN A LAVISH SAUCE.**

There is no shortage of salad vegetables either. Even a simple taco would not be complete without the stylish addition of some fresh tomato, lettuce, capsicum, onion and avocado, while pickled and chilled salad vegetables, often topped with grated goat's cheese, toasted garlic bread-crumbs or fresh herbs, are favourite tapas dishes. It was, after all, the Spanish discovery or Mexico and the New World that gave us all tomatoes and the chilli pepper, capsicums, avocados and corn, beans, zucchini and many other varieties of squash.

These cuisines often mix fruit with salad vegetables. Avocado and papaya make a great combination, especially when served with a dressing of freshly squeezed lime juice and olive oil. Invariably a tapas feast will feature a platter of succulent fresh fruit.

In Spanish cities, street vendors meander through the markets and central squares selling ornately cut pineapples, oranges, watermelons and rockmelons. They always have chilli powder, salt, lime juice and salsas on hand, as the Spanish love their fruit laced with chilli!